SNAP REVISION WRITING
(for papers 1 and 2)

AQA GCSE 9-1 English Language

AQA GCSE 9-1
ENGLISH
LANGUAGE

REVISE TRICKY TOPICS IN A SNAP

English Contents

Published by Collins
An imprint of HarperCollins*Publishers*
1 London Bridge Street,
London, SE1 9GF

© HarperCollins*Publishers* Limited 2017

9780008242336

First published 2017

10 9 8

British Library Cataloguing in Publication Data.
A CIP record of this book is available from the British Library.
Printed in Great Britain by Martins the Printers

ACKNOWLEDGEMENTS
The author and publisher are grateful to the copyright holders for permission to use quoted materials and images.

All images are © Shutterstock.com

Every effort has been made to trace copyright holders and obtain their permission for the use of copyright material. The author and publisher will gladly receive information enabling them to rectify any error or omission in subsequent editions. All facts are correct at time of going to press.

How To Use This Book

To get the most out of this revision guide, just work your way through the book in the order it is presented.

This is how it works:

Revise

Clear and concise revision notes help you get to grips with the topic

Revise

Key Points and Key Words explain the important information you need to know

Revise

A Quick Test at the end of every topic is a great way to check your understanding

Practise

Practice questions for each topic reinforce the revision content you have covered

Review

The Review section is a chance to revisit the topic to improve your recall in the exam

Spelling

You must be able to:

- Spell basic and regular words
- Spell complex and irregular words.

Spelling Rules

- A lot of English spelling is regular, meaning it follows rules or patterns. Here are some of the most useful rules.

'i' before 'e' except after 'c'
- achieve
- receive

Changing the 'y' to 'ie'
- Change the 'y' to 'ie' when adding 's' to a word ending in 'y'.
  - berry – berries
  - pity – pities
  but only if there is a **consonant** before the 'y'. If there is a **vowel** before the 'y', you just add 's'.
  - boy – boys
  - say – says
- Follow the same rule when you add 'ed'.
  - pity – pitied
  - play – played

- To form the **plural** of words that end in 'o', add 'es' (potatoes), except for words taken from Italian (pianos).
- If a word ends in 's' or a 'buzzing' or 'hissing' sound, add 'es' (glasses, dashes).
- You can also learn when to double a letter before 'ing' or 'ed'.
- Look for other patterns and rules that will help your spelling and learn them.

Homophones

- **Homophones** are words that sound the same but have different meanings. These cause a lot of problems. Here are some of the most common:
  - 'Here' means 'in this place': 'It's over here.'
  - You hear with your ears: 'I can hear you.'
  - 'There' means 'in that place': 'I put it over there.' It is also used in phrases such as 'there is' and 'there are'.
  - 'They're' is a **contraction** of 'they are': 'They're not really friends.'
  - 'Their' means 'belonging to them': 'They took all their things with them.'
  - 'Where', like 'here' and 'there', refers to place: 'Where do you think you're going?'

- 'Wear' is used about clothes etc.: 'You wear your earrings on your ears'.
- 'We're and 'were' are not homophones but they often get mixed up:
  * 'We're' is a contraction of 'we are': 'We're in the same class.'
  * 'Were' is the **past tense** of 'are': 'We were very happy there.'
- 'To' indicates direction: 'He went to the cinema.' It is also used as part of a **verb**: 'I want to do this now.'
- 'Too' means excessively: 'Too much' or 'too many'.
- 'Two' is the number 2: 'There were two questions to choose from.'

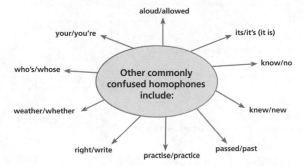

aloud/allowed
your/you're
its/it's (it is)
who's/whose
know/no
Other commonly confused homophones include:
weather/whether
knew/new
right/write
practise/practice
passed/past

- If you're not sure about any of these, look up their meanings and practise using them in sentences. You might be able to think of others that give you trouble.

Spelling Strategies

- **Mnemonics** are ways of remembering things. It can be useful to learn a phrase where the first letters of the words spell out the word you are trying to spell:
  - Big Elephants Can Always Upset Small Elephants (**because**).
- Another useful trick is to **isolate** the part of the word that causes you trouble:
  - There is a **rat** in sep**a**rate.
- Or you might **associate** the spelling with the meaning of the word:
  - **Necessary** – it is necessary to wear one collar, two socks
- Some letters are not pronounced clearly, if at all (**silent letters**).
- Try splitting up the word and saying it slowly and carefully to yourself:
  - **en-vir-on-ment**
  - **k-now-ledge**.

Key Words

consonant
vowel
plural
homophone
contraction
past tense
verb
mnemonic
isolate
associate
silent letter

Punctuation

You must be able to:

- Clearly demarcate sentences
- Accurately use a range of punctuation.

Ending Sentences

- **Full stops** separate sentences. A common mistake students make is to use **commas** instead of full stops.
- **Question marks** can be used in direct speech or at the end of rhetorical questions:
    - 'Do you really want to do that?' she asked.
    - Are we ready to meet the challenge?
- **Exclamation marks** are used to show surprise, shock and other extreme emotions:
    - What a monstrosity!
    - That's amazing!

Commas

- Commas are used to separate subordinate clauses from main clauses. Subordinate clauses give extra information but are not necessary for the sentence to make sense:
    - Mina, having run the marathon, was exhausted. ◄────   'having run the marathon' is the subordinate clause
    - After eating two puddings, Ali was full. ◄────   'After eating two puddings' is the subordinate clause
- They are used in lists:
    - I ordered fish, chips, mushy peas and a fizzy drink.
- Commas are also used to introduce and to end direct speech:
    - He shouted, 'Leave me alone!'
    - 'Nobody move,' ordered the policeman.

Colons and Semi-colons

- **Colons** are used before an explanation:
    - It took two hours: it was a difficult job.
- They introduce quotations:
    - Mercutio plays down his injury: 'Ay, ay, a scratch, a scratch.'
- They introduce lists:
    - The collection was wide and varied: historic manuscripts; suits of armour; ancient bones; and hundreds of old coins.
- Note that **semi-colons** are used to separate the items in the list above. Semi-colons separate list items that consist of more than one or two words. The semi-colon helps with clarity.
- Semi-colons are also used to show that two clauses are closely related, when the writer does not want to use a connective or a full stop:
    - The flowers are blooming; the trees are green.

Key Point

Commas must not be used to link clauses (statements which could stand alone as sentences) unless a connective or relative pronoun is used:

I fed the cat, although it had already eaten.

I fed the cat, which had already eaten.

Brackets, Dashes and Ellipsis

- Brackets (**parentheses**) go around a bit of extra information:
  - A huge man (he was at least seven feet tall) dashed across the road.
- Dashes can be used to show an interruption in the train of thought:
  - I finished the meal – if you could call it that – and quickly left.
- **Ellipsis** (…) indicates the omission of words from a sentence. It can be used to show a thought trailing off or to make the reader wonder what comes next:
  - I realized that I was not alone…

Inverted Commas

- **Inverted commas** can also be referred to as **speech marks** or **quotation marks**.
- Speech marks surround the actual words spoken:
  - 'Never again!' she cried.
- Similarly, when quoting from a text, you put the inverted commas (quotation marks) around any words taken from the original:
  - Tybalt refers to Romeo as 'that villain'.
- Inverted commas are also used for titles:
  - Shelley's 'Ozymandias' is about power.

Apostrophes

- **Apostrophes** are used to show **omission** (also called contraction), or **possession**.
- Only use apostrophes for omission when writing informally. In formal writing you should write all words in full. When you do use an apostrophe, put it where the missing letter or letters would have been:
  - You **shouldn't** have done that.
  - **Malik's** finished but **Rachel's** still working.
  - Let's go home.
- Apostrophes for possession show ownership. If the owner is singular, or a plural that does not end in 's', add an apostrophe and an 's' to the word that indicates the 'owner':
  - the cat's tail
  - the class's teacher
  - the children's toys
  - James's hat.
- The only time you have to do anything different is for a plural ending in 's'. In this case, simply add an apostrophe:
  - the cats' tails
  - the boys' team.

> ### Key Point
>
> Punctuation matters because writing does not make sense without it. Incorrect punctuation can change the meaning of your writing or even turn it into nonsense, confusing the reader.

> ### Key Words
>
> **full stop**
> **comma**
> **question mark**
> **exclamation mark**
> **colon**
> **semi-colon**
> **parenthesis**
> **ellipsis**
> **inverted commas**
> **speech marks**
> **quotation marks**
> **apostrophe**
> **omission**
> **possession**

Quick Test

Insert the correct punctuation:
1. Wheres my hamster Leo cried
2. He had gone there was no doubt about it
3. Maureen who lived next door searched her bins
4. Maureens son found Hammy in the kitchen

Sentence Structure

You must be able to:

- Use sentence structures accurately
- Use a variety of sentence structures for effect.

Simple Sentences

- Every sentence must contain a **subject** and a main verb. The subject is the person or thing (a **noun**) that the sentence is about. The verb is the doing, feeling or being word:

  Ronnie ate
  subject   verb

- **Simple sentences** often include an **object** (also a noun).

  Ronnie ate an apple
  subject   verb   object

  'An apple' is the direct object. You can also use an indirect object:

  Ronnie ate at the table
  subject   verb   preposition   object

  The **preposition** explains Ronnie's relationship to the table.
- You can vary simple sentences, and other sentence forms, by changing the verb from the **active** to the **passive voice**:

  The apple was eaten by Ronnie
  subject   verb   preposition   agent

  Here the apple, by being put at the start of the sentence, becomes the subject.

Minor Sentences

- A **minor sentence**, also known as a **fragment**, is not really a sentence at all because it does not contain a main verb. These are very short and are used for effect. They are often answers to questions or exclamations:
  - Oh my word!
  - Just another boring day.
- They should be used rarely or they will lose their impact.

Compound Sentences

- To make a **compound sentence** you join together two **clauses** of equal importance using a **conjunction**. Clauses are phrases that could stand alone as simple sentences.
- You can use 'and', 'but' or 'or' to form compound sentences:
  - Lucia left the room and [she] went to the shops.
  - Lucia left the room but Mark stayed in the house.

 Key Point

Try to vary the length and type of sentences you use. The examiner is looking for a range of sentence types being used.

- You can join more than two clauses in this way, though the result often appears clumsy:
  - Lucia left the room and went to the shops and bought a banana.

Complex Sentences

- A **complex sentence** also has two or more clauses joined together. The main clause should make sense on its own but the **subordinate clause**, which adds detail or explanation, does not need to.
- Some complex sentences are formed by joining two clauses with a conjunction. In these sentences the two clauses are not equal. Examples of conjunctions you might use are:

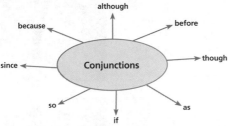

- The conjunction tells you what the relationship between the two clauses is:
  - Charlie left school **because** he had moved house.
  - Charlie left home **after** he had moved house.

  In the first sentence moving house is the reason for Charlie leaving school, whereas the second simply tells us the order in which the events happened.
- Sometimes the conjunction is placed at the beginning of the sentence rather than between the two clauses:
  - Although he felt ill, Dan ate an apple.
- Conjunctions are not needed to form complex sentences:
  - Maria, who loved shopping, left the house immediately.
  - Having left the house quickly, Maria went shopping.
- The first of these examples uses a **relative pronoun** (who) to connect the clauses, while the second changes the verb form to a past participle (having left).
- You can build even longer sentences by using several clauses and joining them in an appropriate way:
  - Dan was ill for several days so he stayed in bed, sometimes reading and sometimes watching television, but mostly bored and grumpy.

> ## Key Point
>
> Complex sentences can give more information and express more complex ideas.

Key Words

subject
noun
simple sentence
object
preposition
active voice
passive voice
minor sentence
fragment
compound sentence
clause
conjunction
complex sentence
subordinate clause
relative pronoun

Quick Test

Which of the following is (a) a simple sentence, (b) a compound sentence, (c) a complex sentence and (d) a minor sentence?
1. Never again.
2. The hamster was found safe and well.
3. She liked sheep but she hated cows.
4. Although she had been there before, the girl could not remember where she was.

Text Structure and Organization

You must be able to:

- Organize your writing in coherent paragraphs
- Use a range of discourse markers.

Paragraphs

- The traditional way of starting a new **paragraph** is to **indent** the first line of the new paragraph, that is, start a centimetre or two in from your margin. This is usual in most books, and in handwritten work. Try to do it in your exams.
- There is no set length for paragraphs. Try to vary the length of your paragraphs. You might use long paragraphs for a detailed description or explanation and short paragraphs for impact.

Starting a New Paragraph

- When you start writing about something new, you should start a new paragraph. This could be a change of:
  - **speaker** – when using direct speech, start a new paragraph when a new person speaks:

    'I didn't see anything,' added Marco.

  - **person** – introducing a new character:

    Julie was quite the opposite…

  - **place**:

    Toppington is also worth a visit…

  - **time**:

    A week later, Roland realized that all was not well…

  - **topic or idea** – moving from one aspect of your subject to another or introducing a different opinion:

    Another cause of concern is the local bus shelter…
    Some residents disagree with this view…

- Paragraphs often start with **topic sentences**, which introduce the topic or subject of the paragraph:

  When we left, there was nobody else on the boat.

  Laurie Grantham, 17, has her own take on fashion.

> **Key Point**
>
> Paragraphs help you to organize your text so that it makes sense, follows a logical order and is easier to read.

← The topic of the paragraph is the boat and whether or not it was empty.

← This paragraph is about Laurie's attitude to fashion.

Opening and Closing Paragraphs

- Opening and closing paragraphs can make a big difference to the impact of your writing. How you approach them depends on the form and purpose of your writing.
- Beginnings and endings in descriptive and narrative writing are dealt with on pages 18–21. Beginnings and endings in non-fiction are dealt with on pages 23–25.

Discourse Markers

- **Discourse markers** connect sentences and paragraphs. They guide readers through the text, showing how one sentence relates to another and how one paragraph relates to another.
- They can be single-word **connectives**, such as 'however', or phrases, such as 'in addition to this'. A discourse marker can also be a phrase which picks up on an idea from the previous paragraph:
  - This kind of behaviour is common throughout Europe.
- Not all discourse markers (for example, 'however' and 'therefore') have to be used at the beginning of a sentence. They can be more effective a little way in.
- Discourse markers have many different purposes:

To add information or ideas	In addition; As well as; Furthermore; Moreover	The new building, moreover, will ruin the view from Huntington Hill.
To point out a similarity	Similarly; In the same way	Similarly, the owl hunts at night.
To introduce a contrasting idea or point of view	Nevertheless; On the other hand; In spite of; Alternatively	Some good points have been made in favour of the plan. Nevertheless, I still think it's a bad idea.
To express cause and effect	As a result; Consequently; In order to; Therefore	I have had no objections so far. I will, therefore, continue as planned.
To give order or to sum up	Firstly; Finally; In conclusion; Basically	Finally, I'd like to thank Josh for making all this possible.
To express passing time	Subsequently; Later; As soon as; Meanwhile	The police took an hour to arrive. Meanwhile, Archie had escaped.

> **Key Point**
>
> You do not have to use a discourse marker in every sentence or even every paragraph, especially in descriptive and narrative writing.

Quick Test

Identify the discourse markers in the following sentences and explain their purpose.
1. First, I will consider Ken's proposal.
2. Tom's idea, on the other hand, is ridiculous.
3. Before the bus shelter was built, there was no vandalism.
4. I suggest, therefore, that we demolish the bus shelter.

Key Words

paragraph
indent
topic sentence
discourse marker
connective

Standard English and Grammar

You must be able to:

- Use Standard English
- Use correct grammatical structures.

Standard English

- **Standard English** is the version of English that is widely accepted as being correct.
- You may not always have to write in Standard English. Characters in a story might use **dialect** or **slang**. If you are writing for teenagers or children, you might use the sort of language they would use with their friends.
- For all other purposes write in Standard English, using correct **grammar** and spelling.

Personal Pronouns: First Person

- The most common misuse of **personal pronouns** is the confusion of 'I' and 'me'. 'I' is the subject of the sentence; 'me' is the object:
  - 'Ikram and me were late' is clearly wrong because you would not say: 'Me was late.' You would say: 'I was late.' So, logically, it must be: 'Ikram and I were late.'
  - Similarly you should not say: 'They gave prizes to Lucy and I.' The correct form is: 'They gave prizes to Lucy and me.'

Personal Pronouns: Second Person

- 'You' is both the **singular** and **plural** form of the second person. You could say, 'Thank you for coming' to one person or to hundreds. There is no such word as 'yous'.
- Do not use the Americanism 'you guys'. 'Guys' is not Standard English.

Words and Phrases to Avoid

- Be aware of any words or phrases that are common in your area but are not Standard English, and avoid using them in formal writing.
- The same applies to current slang used by young people (such as 'sick' for 'good') and Americanisms, for example, using 'lay' instead of 'lie' or 'period' rather than 'full stop'.

Modal Verbs

- Do not use the word 'of' instead of 'have' after **modal verbs** such as would, could, should and might:
  - If I'd known, I would **have** told you.

> **Key Point**
>
> Standard English is the form of English which is most widely understood. You need to be able to use it so that your audience can understand what you are saying.

Verbs: Agreement and Tenses

- There are three basic tenses – past, **present** and future. This section focuses on the past tense because that is where most errors occur.
  - A common error is to confuse the first and **third person** of the verb, for example, using 'you was' instead of 'you were'.
  - Another is the confusion of the **simple past tense** and the **perfect tense**, which expresses a completed action (for example, using 'done' instead of 'did' or 'has done'). The perfect tense is formed by adding the past participle to 'have' or 'has'.
- Most verbs follow this pattern:

	Singular	Plural
Simple past	I/you/he/she/it walked.	We/you/they walked.
Perfect	I/you have walked. He/she/it has walked.	We/you/they have walked.

> **Key Point**
>
> The subject and verb of your sentence must agree in number and person.

- Many of the most commonly used verbs are irregular, among them the verb 'to be'. These are its correct forms:

	Singular	Plural
Simple past	I was.	We were.
	You were.	You were.
	He/she/it was.	They were.
Perfect	I/you have been.	We/you have been.
	He/she/it has been.	They have been.

- Some other irregular verbs which cause problems are shown here.

Simple Past	Perfect	Simple Past	Perfect
ate	have/has eaten	sang	has/has sung
did	have/has done	saw	have/has seen
drove	have/has driven	spoke	have/has spoken
gave	have/has given	taught	have/has taught
got	have/has got	went	have/has gone
lay	have/has lain	woke	have/has woken

- If you are writing in the past tense and you want to refer to something that happened before the events you are describing, use the **past perfect tense**, which is formed using 'had' and the past participle:
  - She had eaten before she arrived.
- If you are writing about an event in the past which continued for some time, use the **past continuous**, formed by the past tense of the verb 'to be' and the present participle:
  - She was eating for the whole journey.

> **Key Words**
>
> **Standard English**
> **dialect**
> **slang**
> **grammar**
> **personal pronoun**
> **singular**
> **plural**
> **modal verb**
> **present tense**
> **third person**
> **simple past tense**
> **perfect tense**
> **past perfect tense**
> **past continuous tense**

> **Quick Test**
>
> Rewrite the following sentences in Standard English:
> 1. Me and Jay was put on detention.
> 2. I seen you guys on Saturday.
> 3. You was the bestest player we had.
> 4. After we had sang the first number, we done a dance.

1 The following paragraph includes 10 incorrect spellings. Find them and rewrite them correctly.

> We where hoping for good whether for Sports Day. Unfortunately, on Friday morning it was poring with rain. Luckily, by ten o'clock it was clear and sunny. I was very exited when I got to the stadium but I had a long weight for my race, the 200 meters. Their were eight of us in the final. I was in the inside lane, witch I don't usually like, but I ran well round the bend and was second comming into the straight. As I crossed the line I was neck and neck with Jo. It wasn't until the teacher congratulated me that I knew I had definately won.

_____

_____ [10]

2 The following five sentences have been written without punctuation.
Insert the correct punctuation.

a) Peter Kowalski who was the tallest boy in the class easily won the high jump.

_____

b) What are you doing in the sand pit shouted Miss O'Connor get out of there at once.

_____

c) Francesca won medals for the long jump the high jump and the relay.

_____

d) I wasnt entered in any of the races because Im hopeless at running.

_____

e) Jonathan finished last however he was pleased with his time.

_____ [5]

3 **a)** Change each of the following pairs of sentences into single sentences, using conjunctions.

i) Julia stayed off school. She had a stomach ache.

_____

ii) He might be in the changing rooms. He might have already left.

_____

b) Change the following pairs of sentences into single sentences using relative pronouns.

i) Michael announced the results. He has a really loud voice.

_____

ii) The form with the best results won a cup. The cup was presented by Mr Cadogan.

_____

c) Turn the following three sentences into a single sentence.

   i) Maria had won the discus competition. She went home early. She was feeling sick.

   _____ [5]

4 Rewrite the following sentences using Standard English.

a) Me and Hayley is going to town tomorrow.

   _____

b) You guys can come wiv us if youse want.

   _____

c) We was well chuffed with what we bought.

   _____

d) I don't know nothing about what they done at school.

   _____

e) I aint skiving off again coz I wanna get my GCSEs.

   _____ [5]

5 Insert each of the following five connectives or discourse markers in the text below to help it to make sense.

however   **as well as**   **also**   **as a result of**   **consequently**

I am disgusted by the plan to close our library. (1)_____ having a massive impact on our community, this act of vandalism shows how little interest the council has in education. (2) _____ this attitude, our children are being deprived of a wonderful resource. Adults, especially older people, (3) _____ benefit greatly from the library. The council says we can use Hartington Library, but that is much too far away for most pensioners. (4) _____, they will lose what has become for many a real lifeline, making them feel part of the community. (5) _____, it does not have to be like this. There are other ways for the council to save money: we could start with cutting down on the Mayor's free trips to America! [5]

6 Rewrite the following paragraph on a separate piece of paper, correcting errors in spelling, punctuation and grammar.

My first experiance of Bingley Park Library was when I was five. My grandmother, who were an avid reader, visitted the library every week and always borrowed four books. She read more or less anything but she especially liked detective story's, gardening books, and film star's biografies. Naturally, she wanted the rest of her family to be as enthusiastic as she was about books therefore, as soon as I could read, me and her marched down to bingley park. It was an imposing and rather frightening edifice for a child of five, the librarian, Miss Maloney, was just as imposing and twice as intimidating. [10]

Practice Questions

1   Insert the correctly spelled word in each of the following pairs of sentences.

    a) except/accept

        I did them all _____ the last one.

        I _____ your apology.

    b) affect/effect

        The weather seemed to have a bad _____ on everyone's mood.

        I don't think the weather will _____ the result.

    c) aloud/allowed

        Nobody is _____ in here at lunchtime.

        Mo really likes reading _____ in class.

    d) write/right

        Nobody got the _____ answer.

        I'll _____ a letter and explain.

    e) who's/whose

        He couldn't return it because he didn't know _____ coat it was.

        Tell me _____ going and then I'll decide.   **[5]**

2   Rewrite the following passage on a separate piece of paper using the correct punctuation.

> dont you think we should wait for him asked Eve
>
> not at all Henry replied he never waits for us
>
> well that's true Eve replied but he doesn't know the way

        [10]

3   Rewrite the following passage on a separate piece of paper, using a variety of simple, compound and complex sentences (and adding words if necessary) to make it more effective.   **[10]**

> Henry and Eve waited for another ten minutes. Joel did not arrive. They left without him. They walked to the bus stop. There was no-one there. This suggested they had just missed the bus. Henry was very annoyed with Joel. Eve told him to calm down. She told him to forget about Joel. The journey was uneventful. They got off the bus by the lake. It looked eerie in the moonlight. They sat down on a grassy bank. They took their sandwiches and drinks out of the bag. Henry felt a hand on his shoulder.

        [10]

4   Pick the five sentences in which the correct forms of the verb are used.

    a) You was really good tonight.   ☐

    b) Ms Greenall taught me how to boil an egg.   ☐

c) They've gotten two more kittens. ☐

d) I knew the song because we had sung it in class. ☐

e) I rung the bell twice but nobody come. ☐

f) She lay on the sofa until she felt better. ☐

g) I done my homework at break. ☐

h) He says he won't come because he's already seen it. ☐

i) I have done what you asked. ☐

j) I'm going to lay down here for a while. ☐ [5]

5 Put the following nouns into their plural forms.

a) pizza _____

b) latch _____

c) mosquito _____

d) sheep _____

e) donkey _____

f) stadium _____

g) quality _____

h) church _____

i) woman _____

j) hypothesis _____ [5]

6 Rearrange the following paragraphs so that the whole letter makes sense.

a) The next thing I knew two young girls were leaning over me. I'm sorry to say I thought the worst when I saw the rings through their noses. But they asked me if I was all right and very gently helped me to stand up. One of them stayed with me while the other went into the shop and fetched a chair. Then I noticed there were two boys carefully collecting all my shopping and bagging it up.

b) When it was all collected in, they called a taxi to take me home. I'm sorry to say I didn't ask their names, so I'd like to give them a big thank you through your newspaper. Whoever you are, you're a real credit to Bilberry and to your generation!

c) I was in town on Wednesday to do my usual shop in the supermarket. I got a little more than usual so my bags were rather heavy. As I came out of the shop I lost my balance and keeled over, spilling all my shopping.

d) I wasn't badly hurt but it was quite a shock. I just sat there on the pavement, stunned and not knowing what to do.

e) I am writing to express my thanks to a group of young people I met last week. It isn't often we hear good things about teenagers. We read so much about crime and vandalism, drinking and bad manners that we can easily end up thinking the worst of all teenagers.

a) ☐ **b)** ☐ **c)** ☐ **d)** ☐ **e)** ☐ [5]

Narrative Writing

You must be able to:

- Write clear and imaginative narratives.

Narrative

- A **narrative** is an account of events – a story, whether real or imagined.
- One of the writing tasks in Paper 1 will ask you to write a story or part of a story. This gives you the opportunity to use your imagination and be creative.
- You may be asked to write for a particular audience. If so, it is most likely to be for people of your own age.
- You will be given a 'stimulus' for your story. This could be a picture or just a brief instruction:
  - Write the opening of a story suggested by the picture above.
  - Write a story about someone whose life changes suddenly.
  These instructions are deliberately vague, so you can develop your own ideas in your own style.

Planning

- Before you start to write, spend a few minutes planning, making decisions about the main elements of your story.

Character and Voice

- Decide whether you are going to write in the first or third person. If you opt for the first person, is the narrator the **protagonist** or an observer?

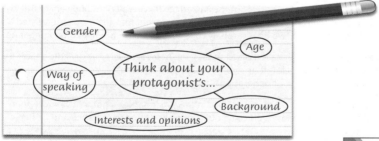

Think about your protagonist's...
- Gender
- Age
- Background
- Interests and opinions
- Way of speaking

- The protagonist could be a version of you, but it can be much more interesting to write about someone who is completely different.
- There may also be an **antagonist**, someone who stands in the way of or opposes the protagonist.
- Think about other, minor characters – but beware of inventing too many. You don't want to make things too complicated.

Key Point

You can tell a story in your own voice or you can invent a character (persona) to tell the story.

Structure

- The same applies to the plot. If you are writing a complete story, keep it fairly simple.
  - You need an inciting incident, a climax and at least one turning point, but not too many.
  - You need to establish your 'world,' but don't spend too much time on exposition.
  - You might end with a shock or surprise. It has been said that writers should give their readers what they want but not in the way they expect.
- If you are only writing the opening, make sure something interesting or dramatic happens that would make a reader want to know what happens in the rest of the story. You should know how the story would develop and end.
- It is less likely that you would be asked to write the end of a story, but if you are asked to do this, you need to know what happened before the point at which you start your story.
- Stories are normally written mainly in chronological order but you might want to use 'flashbacks'.

Language and Style

- Normally you would write in Standard English but if you use a first-person narrator, you should write in that person's **voice**. Think about its tone – formal or chatty? – as well as whether to use dialect or slang.
- Stories are usually written in the past tense. Using the present tense can make the action seem more immediate and vivid, though. You can use either, but stick to one.
- **Direct speech** can help to move on the story and tell us about character, but use it sparingly. Think about whether it adds anything – and make sure you set it out properly. Sometimes **indirect** (or **reported**) **speech** can be more effective.
- Write in paragraphs. These should usually be linked by discourse markers, particularly ones that relate to time:
  - After they left, he sank to his knees.
- Use a variety of sentence structures, for example using complex sentences for descriptions and simple or even minor sentences for dramatic impact:
  - It was her.
  - A gun beneath the leaves.
- Use a range of punctuation but avoid using a lot of exclamation marks.

> ### Key Point
>
> Be careful not to just tell the 'bare bones' of the story. You also need to describe people and places.

Key Words

narrative
protagonist
antagonist
voice
direct speech
indirect speech
reported speech

Quick Test

What is meant by the following?
1. The protagonist.
2. The antagonist.
3. The inciting incident.
4. A turning point.

Descriptive Writing

You must be able to:

- Write clear and imaginative descriptions.

Description

- One of the tasks in Paper 1 will be to write a description, possibly based on a picture. If there is a picture, you are not limited to describing what is actually in the picture. It is there to stimulate your imagination.
- When writing a description you can draw on your memories of real people, places or things.
- You might also be inspired by something you've read.
- Think about different aspects of your subject – and not just positive ones. This is especially important when describing a person – there is only so much you can write about how lovely someone is.
- Think about all five senses: sight, hearing, smell, taste and touch. When you have decided what you want to describe, it is a good idea to jot down what you experience through each sense. If you were describing a beach you might put:

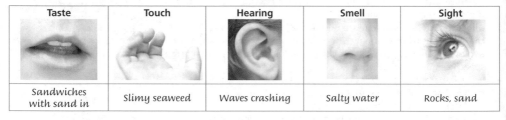

Taste	Touch	Hearing	Smell	Sight
Sandwiches with sand in	Slimy seaweed	Waves crashing	Salty water	Rocks, sand

- Another useful way of approaching description is 'big to small', starting with what something is like from a distance and moving in like a camera:

| the panoramic view | → | sand, rocks and people | → | children playing in rock pool | → | shells and seaweed |

Language and Style

- Consider whether to use the first or third person – you may or may not want to describe personal feelings:

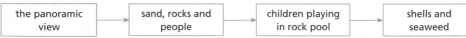

    I feel a huge sense of regret as the train leaves.

- Decide whether to write in the present or past tense: they can be equally effective but you should stick to one.
- Use **imagery** and figurative language, including metaphors and similes:

    The train roared like an angry lion.

> ### Key Point
>
> When you describe something, remember that you can use all five senses.

- Use adjectives and adverbs:

  - The deep mysterious sea
  - The engine spluttered fitfully.

- Be adventurous in your choice of vocabulary. Use words that have precise, rather than general, meanings. Does the man walk across the road? Or does he amble, trot, stride or even swagger?
- Use techniques such as alliteration, assonance and onomatopoeia:

  - sparkling, shining sea
  - gloomy blue rooms
  - the fizz and pop of the fireworks

- Use both active and passive voices:

  - A dark forest surrounded the cottage.
  - The cottage is surrounded by a dark forest.

- Write in paragraphs. Vary their length and link them with a variety of discourse markers:

  - Beyond this lies a flat, wide bog.
  - But these sights were as nothing to what lay beyond.

> **Key Point**
>
> If the task is to write a description, do not write a story.

- Vary your sentence lengths and use techniques such as **parallel phrasing**. This is the use of phrases constructed in the same way and arranged in pairs or sequences:

  - Tiny rivulets run down the lane; a massive lake covers the fields.

Example

- This description of a person uses some of the techniques described above.

George lived alone. Gnarled and weather-beaten, he looked older than his sixty years: his skin was sun-baked and blemished; his forehead grooved with deep furrows; his few remaining teeth black and crooked, like ancient gravestones. His teeth were rarely seen, for he had few reasons to smile. His one companion was his terrier Barney, whom he loved. In return Barney offered unquestioning love, loyalty and apparent affection.

It is written in the past tense and the third person.

It describes George's appearance but also gives us some background.

The imagery is mainly literal but figurative imagery is also used.

Both active and passive voices are used.

There is a variety of sentence structures.

Look at the example above. Find examples of:
1. A simple sentence.
2. A simile.
3. Alliteration.
4. The passive voice.

> **Key Words**
>
> imagery
> parallel phrasing

Writing Non-fiction 1

You must be able to:

- Communicate clearly, effectively and imaginatively
- Adapt your writing for different forms, purposes and audiences.

The Task

- Paper 2 of the English Language exam includes one writing task. It gives you the opportunity to express your views on a theme explored in the reading section of the exam.
- You will be given a statement or scenario, and instructions which include details of purpose, form and audience:

> School holidays create problems for parents and damage children's education.
>
> Write an article for a student website in which you argue for or against this view.

Audience

- Sometimes the task specifies an **audience**:

> Write a letter to your head teacher.

- Sometimes the audience is implied by the form:

> – Write an article for your school website.

- Your intended audience determines what sort of language you use. Think about whether a formal or informal tone is called for.
- You would write informally for people you know well, using the sort of language that you use when chatting with them. However, you should avoid using 'text language' (**abbreviations**, emoticons etc.) in the exam.
- It can be appropriate to write informally for people you don't know, as if you were their friend, for example, in a magazine article aimed at teenagers.
- For almost everything else use a formal tone and write in Standard English (see pages 12–13).
- Whether you are writing formally or informally, be aware of your audience's interests and points of view. For example, if you were writing for a local audience you would focus on known local concerns:

> Here in Bingley, we have always been proud of our green spaces.

- – You would expect school governors to be concerned about the school's reputation:

> I know that you are just as concerned as I am about recent complaints of unsocial behaviour.

> **Key Point**
>
> You are free to agree or disagree with the stimulus you are given. The important thing is to try to convince the reader of your view.

– And a little flattery can go a long way:

I have always been impressed by your commitment to our community.

Purpose

- The purpose of your writing is to express your point of view. The wording of the task might give a slightly different emphasis. For example, 'argue' sounds more passionate than 'explain', while 'persuade' suggests more emphasis on the audience.

Constructing Your Argument

- In constructing your **argument**, start with a powerful opening paragraph, which grabs your audience and makes your point clear.
- Make sure you offer a number of points in support of your argument, starting a new paragraph for each.
- Acknowledge other points of view but then give your **counter-arguments**, pointing out why you think they are wrong:

Some people argue that school uniforms stifle individuality. However,...

- Structure your argument in a logical order, using **discourse markers** to 'signpost' the development of your argument:

Another point I would like to make is...

- Back up your points with evidence if you can. You can use the sources for the reading question to help you with this.
- Give appropriate examples, including **anecdotes**:

Only last week, I encountered such behaviour...

- Address your audience directly (**direct address**), using 'you', and show your own involvement by using 'I' and 'we'.
- Use a full range of **rhetorical devices**, including lists of three, repetition and **hyperbole**.
- Use humour if you think it is appropriate.
- Use a variety of sentence structures, and use the passive as well as the active voice.
- Finish with a strong conclusion, summing up the main points and strongly stating your opinion.

> ### Key Point
>
> Spend a few minutes (but only a few!) planning your answer, using whatever method works best for you.

> ### Key Words
>
> audience
> abbreviation
> argument
> counter-argument
> discourse marker
> anecdote
> direct address
> rhetorical device
> hyperbole

Quick Test

Your head teacher has banned packed lunches. You want to write to the governors giving your reaction. What would be the:

1. purpose?
2. audience?
3. form?

Writing Non-fiction 2

You must be able to:

- Communicate clearly, effectively and imaginatively
- Adapt your writing for different forms, purposes and audiences.

Form: Articles

- You could be asked to write an article for a newspaper, magazine or website.
- If it is a newspaper, the task might specify whether it is a **broadsheet**, **tabloid** or local newspaper.
- Broadsheets are 'serious' newspapers, which look at news in more detail and depth, such as the *Daily Telegraph* and *The Guardian*.
- Tabloids, like *The Sun* and the *Daily Mirror*, cover news in less depth and devote more space to things like celebrity gossip.
- Tabloids use short paragraphs and sentences, and simple vocabulary. Broadsheets use longer paragraphs and sentences, and more sophisticated vocabulary.
- Do not try to make your answer look like a newspaper or magazine. There are no marks for design. Do not include:
  - a masthead (the newspaper's title)
  - columns
  - illustrations
  - any articles apart from the one you have been asked to write.
- You can, however, include organizational devices such as:
  - a **headline** – perhaps using alliteration ('Ban this Beastly Business'), a **pun** or a play on words ('A Tale of Two Kitties'). But don't put it in huge coloured letters!
  - a **strapline**, under the headline, expanding on or explaining the headline ('Why We Should Boycott Cosmetics')
  - **subheadings** – to guide the reader through the text.
- You must write in paragraphs.
- Magazine and website articles are similar to newspaper articles in form.

> ### Key Point
>
> You are not likely to be asked to write a tabloid article: it would not give you enough scope to demonstrate your skills.

Form: Letters

- There are a number of 'rules' or conventions that are used in letter-writing. These are often not used in informal letters.
- If you are asked to write a letter in the exam, it will probably be quite formal.

Example of How to Open a Letter

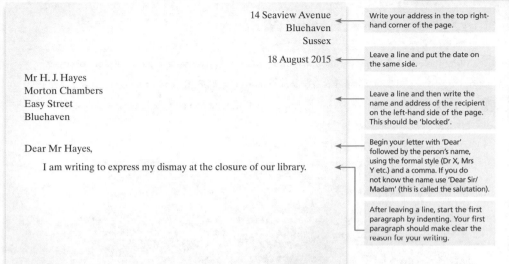

14 Seaview Avenue
Bluehaven
Sussex

Write your address in the top right-hand corner of the page.

18 August 2015

Leave a line and put the date on the same side.

Mr H. J. Hayes
Morton Chambers
Easy Street
Bluehaven

Leave a line and then write the name and address of the recipient on the left-hand side of the page. This should be 'blocked'.

Dear Mr Hayes,

Begin your letter with 'Dear' followed by the person's name, using the formal style (Dr X, Mrs Y etc.) and a comma. If you do not know the name use 'Dear Sir/Madam' (this is called the salutation).

    I am writing to express my dismay at the closure of our library.

After leaving a line, start the first paragraph by indenting. Your first paragraph should make clear the reason for your writing.

- Continue with paragraphs that make further relevant points before ending with one that tells the reader what you would like to happen next.
- Connect your paragraphs with discourse markers.
- If you have addressed the reader by name, sign off with 'Yours sincerely'. If you haven't, use 'Yours faithfully'.
- Remember the 'five Cs':
  - Clear – Say what you mean in good English.
  - Complete – Include everything necessary, giving enough detail and explaining your points properly.
  - Concise – Don't 'ramble'. Do not include irrelevant information or ideas.
  - Correct – Say what you believe to be true.
  - Courteous – Be polite. Consider the recipient and his or her possible reaction to your letter.

Key Point

Unless you are writing informally for young people, avoid slang or dialect words, contractions and abbreviations.

Quick Test

How should you end a letter beginning with the following salutations?
1. Dear Mr Blenkinsop
2. Dear Principal
3. Dear Madam
4. Dear Sir Arthur

Key Words

broadsheet
tabloid
headline
pun
strapline
subheading

Narrative and Descriptive Writing

1 Write the opening of a story about a mother and her son. Write on a separate piece of paper.

[24 marks for content and organization; 16 marks for technical accuracy; total 40]

2 You are going to enter a creative writing competition, judged by people of your own age.

EITHER

Write a description suggested by this picture.

OR

Write the opening of a story about a student who is doing a holiday job in a shop or cafe.

[24 marks for content and organization; 16 marks for technical accuracy ; total 40]

3 You have been asked to write a creative piece for your school magazine or website.

EITHER

Write a description suggested by this picture.

OR

Write the opening of a story set in a wild, isolated place. Write on a separate piece of paper.

[24 marks for content and organization; 16 marks for technical accuracy; total 40]

4. You are going to enter a creative writing competition.

EITHER

Write a description suggested by this picture.

OR

Write the story of a bus, tram or train journey.

[24 marks for content and organization; 16 marks for technical accuracy ; total 40]

Writing Non-fiction 1 and 2

1 'A dog is for life, not just for Christmas.'

Write an article for a magazine aimed at people your own age, inspired by this quotation, in which you give your views about dogs, dog owners, or both.

Write on a separate piece of paper.

[24 marks for content and organization; 16 marks for technical accuracy; total 40]

2 'School trips are a waste of time and money.'

Write an article for a magazine aimed at people your own age giving your views on this statement.

Write your answer on a separate piece of paper.

[24 marks for content and organization; 16 marks for technical accuracy; total 40]

3 'Travel might broaden the mind, but tourism is destroying some of the world's most beautiful places. It is time we put the good of the planet before our own pleasure.'

Write an article for a broadsheet newspaper in which you explain your point of view on this statement.

[24 marks for content and organization; 16 marks for technical accuracy; total 40]

4 'Libraries are a thing of the past. You can get all the information you need from the internet at home. People who like books can buy them or download them. There are much more important things to spend public money on.'

Write an article for a broadsheet newspaper in which you explain your point of view on this statement.

[24 marks for content and organization; 16 marks for technical accuracy; total 40]

Spelling

1 Put the following words into their plural forms:

a) tomato _____ b) birthday _____

c) soliloquy _____ d) family _____

e) parenthesis _____ [5]

2 Insert the correctly spelled word in each of the following pairs of sentences:

a) **Your/you're**

_____ not going out like that.

I asked _____ sister to bring it.

b) **There/they're/their**

_____ are twenty-five people in the class.

They have all done _____ homework but _____ not sitting in the right places.

c) **Where/wear/we're**

Turn it off or it will _____ out.

We have no idea _____ it is but _____ going anyway.

d) **Past/passed**

I _____ him in the street an hour ago.

He walked right _____ me as if I wasn't there.

e) **To/too/two**

There were only _____ exams _____ sit but that was one _____ many.

f) **Practice/practise**

If you don't go to the _____ you'll be left out of the team.

If you want to improve you will have to _____ every day. [15]

3 The following passage includes ten incorrect spellings. Find them and circle them, then write the correct spellings below.

Last nite I went to the cinema with my friend Bob and his farther, Michael. The whole evening was not very succesfull. The cinema was very crouded and we had to sit seperately. Then, it turned out the film was in a forrein langauge and no-one could understand it. I think it was about the enviroment. Afterwards, Michael took us to a resturant were we had pizzas.

_____

_____

_____

_____

_____ [10]

Total Marks _____ / 30

Punctuation

1 Punctuate the following passage using only commas and full stops. There should be a total of five punctuation marks.

> *Great Expectations* one of the best-known novels by Charles Dickens is the story of Pip a boy who grows up in the marshes of Kent at the beginning of the story he meets an escaped convict in the churchyard where his parents are buried

_____

_____

_____ [5]

2 Add ten apostrophes, where necessary, to the following passage:

> At about ten o clock, we went to Romios for pizzas. Im not sure what Bobs pizza topping was but I had ham and pineapple. I wish I hadnt because later on I was sick in Michaels car. Its brand new and I thought hed be angry but he wasnt. Were not going there again.

_____

_____

_____

_____ [10]

3 Add a question mark, an exclamation mark, a colon, a semi-colon or parentheses (brackets) to the following clauses so that they make sense:

a) Who was that masked man nobody knows.	
b) The cat slept quietly on the mat the dog slept noisily on the step.	
c) I don't believe it that's the first answer I've got.	
d) Annie deserved the prize she was the best baker by far.	
e) Jane and Elizabeth the two oldest Bennet sisters get married at the end.	

[5]

Total Marks _____ / 20

Sentence Structure

1 Identify whether the sentences below are simple, compound, complex or minor sentences:

   a) I confess that I had my doubts when I reflected upon the great traffic which had passed along the London road in the interval. _____

   b) Very clearly. _____

   c) We all need help sometimes. _____

   d) Mr Collins was punctual to his time, and was received with great politeness by the whole family. _____

   e) Elizabeth smiled. _____   [5]

2 Combine the following sentences to form complex sentences, using the conjunctions **because**, **although** or **until**.

   a) I bought Anna a bunch of flowers. It was her birthday.

   _____

   _____

   b) He did not finish the race. They gave him a certificate.

   _____

   _____

   c) I kept going. I reached the finishing line.

   _____

   _____   [3]

3 Use the following sentences to form a complex sentence using a relative pronoun:

   Joey was the oldest cat in the street. He never left the garden.

   _____

   _____

   _____   [1]

4 Use the following sentences to form a complex sentence without using a connective:

   I was walking down the street. I realized I had forgotten my phone.

   _____

   _____

   _____   [1]

Total Marks _____ / 10

Text Structure and Organisation

1 Rearrange the following paragraphs so that the passage makes sense. Write the paragraphs in the correct order below.

a) As a result of this, the student body has decided to appeal to the governors. Jodie has written a letter to every governor, setting out the problems as the students see them.

b) As yet no replies have been received. The increasingly angry students are starting to consider taking 'direct action'.

c) Jodie Collins, a spokesperson for the students, has had several meetings about the issue with the Principal. Ms Rundle apparently listened to the students' points, but later sent an email claiming that nothing can be done because of lack of funds.

d) According to this letter, students' health and safety are at risk. Among other things, toilets are not properly cleaned and standards of hygiene in the kitchen leave a lot to be desired.

e) Students of Summerfield College have expressed concern about the environment they have to work in. They have a number of complaints.

[5]

2 Insert each of these five discourse markers or connectives into the passage so that it makes sense:

nevertheless   when   subsequently   in spite of   however

(a) _____ I read your letter I was shocked by its contents. **(b)** _____ being a governor of the college, I was completely unaware of the issues which you mention.

I have **(c)** _____ been in touch with Ms Rundle to express my concern. She **(d)**, _____, has not responded to my letters. **(e)** _____, I shall continue to press her for answers.

[5]

Total Marks _____ / 10

Standard English and Grammar

1 Insert the correct form of the verb 'to be' or 'to do':

Present tense

a) You _____ a great singer.

b) They _____ trying hard.

Simple past

c) We _____ waiting for you.

d) He _____ what they told him to do.

Perfect

e) She _____ my friend for years.

f) They _____ all their exams now.

Simple past + past perfect

g) We _____ happy because we _____ all the exercises. [7]

2 Which of the following is correct in Standard UK English? Circle the correct word.

a) The defendant **pleaded/pled** guilty.

b) He's one of the **only/few** people who can do that.

c) He has **got/gotten** two coffees. [3]

3 Change the following dialogue to Standard English:

Jo: Hey. How are you guys doing?

Arthur: Good. Real good.

Jo: Wanna drink?

Arthur: Can I get two coffees?

Jo: Sure. Where are you sat?

_____

_____

_____

_____ [5]

4 Rewrite the following passage in Standard English:

> I was stood in the street when Frankie come over. I give him a smile and opened me gob to speak. I was gonna ask him how he done in math. I never said nothing. Soon as I seen him I knew he done good.

_____

_____

_____ [5]

Total Marks _____ / 20

Narrative Writing

Imagine you have been set the following task:

'Write a story about someone who wins a huge amount of money in the lottery.'

Use the following questions and points to help you create a plan for your writing.

1 Character and Voice

    a) What person will you write in? If first person, is the narrator also the protagonist?

    b) What kind of register will the narrator use?

    c) On a separate piece of paper, make notes on your protagonist's:
- gender
- age
- appearance
- background
- relationships
- way of speaking   **[8]**

2 Place and Time

    a) Where does it start?

    b) Does the setting change during the story?

    c) When is it set – now, in the past or in the future?

    d) How long does the story take?

    e) Will it be written in chronological order?

                                                            [5]

3 Structure

On a separate piece of paper, make notes on your:
- exposition
- inciting incident
- turning point(s)
- climax
- coda (ending)   **[5]**

Total Marks _____ / 18

Descriptive Writing

Choose one of the following tasks and answer the questions below:

Either

Describe someone who lives in your street.

Or

Describe a visit to a fairground.

Use the following questions and points to help you create a plan for your writing.

1   **a)** Are you going to use the first or third person? _____

　　　b) Are you going to use the past or present tense? _____   [2]

2   Using an adjective and a noun for each, jot down at least two things you can:

　　　a) see _____

　　　b) hear _____

　　　c) smell _____

　　　d) taste _____

　　　e) touch _____   [10]

3   Make notes on the scene/person from:

　　　a) long distance _____

_____

　　　b) middle distance _____

_____

　　　c) close up _____

_____   [6]

4   Imagery

　　　Write down an appropriate:

　　　a) simile _____

_____

　　　b) metaphor _____

_____   [2]

Total Marks _____ / 20

Writing Non-fiction 1 and 2

1 Imagine you have been asked to give your opinion on the statement 'Work Experience is a complete waste of time and should be abolished'.

Use the table below to list five arguments in favour of abolishing work experience (pro) and five against it (con).

Pros	Cons

[10]

2 The statement above was made in an article in your local newspaper. Decide whether you agree or disagree with it and write only **the opening paragraph** of a letter to the newspaper expressing your view.

[5]

3 Now write only **the opening paragraph** of an article for a teenage magazine expressing your views on the same statement.

[5]

Total Marks _____ / 20

Answers

Page 5 Quick Test
1. no, where.
2. It's.
3. whether, to.
4. practice.

Page 7 Quick Test
1. 'Where's my hamster?' Leo cried.
2. He had gone. There was no doubt about it.
3. Maureen, who lived next door, searched her bins.
4. Maureen's son found Hammy in the kitchen.

Page 9 Quick Test
1. d   2. a   3. b   4. c

Page 11 Quick Test
1. First – to give order.
2. On the other hand – to introduce a contrasting idea or point of view.
3. Before – to express passing time.
4. Therefore – to express cause and effect.

Page 13 Quick Test
1. Jay and I were put on detention.
2. I saw you on Saturday.
3. You were the best player we had.
4. After we had sung the first number, we did a dance.

Page 14
1. were, weather, pouring, excited, wait, metres, There, which, coming, definitely.   **[1 mark for each correct spelling – maximum 10]**
2. a) Peter Kowalski, who was the tallest boy in the class, easily won the high jump.
   b) 'What are you doing in the sand pit?' shouted Miss O'Connor. 'Get out of there at once!'
   c) Francesca won medals for the long jump, the high jump and the relay.
   d) I wasn't entered in any of the races because I'm hopeless at running.
   e) Jonathan finished last. However, he was pleased with his time.
   [1 mark for each sentence – maximum 5]
3. a) (i) Julia stayed off school because she had a stomach ache.
      (ii) He might be in the changing rooms or he might have already left.
   b) (i) Michael, who has a really loud voice, announced the results.
      (ii) The form with the best results won a cup, which was presented by Mr Cadogan.
   c) (i) Maria, who had won the discus competition, went home early because she was feeling sick.
   [1 mark for each – maximum 5]
4. a) Hayley and I are going to town tomorrow.
   b) You can come with us if you want to.
   c) We were very pleased with what we bought.
   d) I do not (don't) know anything about what they did at school.
   e) I am not truanting again because I want to get my GCSEs.
   [1 mark for each – maximum 5]
5. (1) As well as (2) As a result of (3) also (4) Consequently (5) However **[5]**
6. experience **[1]** was **[1]** visited **[1]**] stories **[1]** stars' **[1]** biographies **[1]** Therefore **[1]** she and I **[1]** Bingley Park **[1]** The **[1]**
   [Maximum 10]

Page 16
1. a) except, accept   b) effect, affect
   c) allowed, aloud   d) right, write
   e) whose, who's   **[1 mark for each pair – maximum 5]**
2. 'Don't you think we should wait for him?' asked Eve.
   'Not at all,' Henry replied. 'He never waits for us.'
   'Well, that's true,' Eve replied, 'but he doesn't know the way.'
   [½ mark for each correct punctuation mark – maximum 10]
3. This is a suggested answer only. There are other ways of doing it: Henry and Eve waited for another ten minutes but Joel did not arrive, so they left without him and walked to the bus stop. There was no-one there, suggesting they had just missed the bus. Henry was very annoyed with Joel. However, Eve told him to calm down and forget about Joel. After an uneventful journey, they got off the bus by the lake, which looked eerie in the moonlight. Having sat down on a grassy bank, they took their sandwiches and drinks out of the bag. Henry felt a hand on his shoulder.   **[Maximum 10 marks]**
4. b, d, f, h, i   **[Maximum 5 marks]**
5. a) pizzas   b) latches   c) mosquitoes
   d) sheep   e) donkeys   f) stadia
   g) qualities   h) churches   i) women
   j) hypotheses   **[½ mark for each – maximum 5]**
6. e, c, d, a, b **[Maximum 5 marks]**

Page 19 Quick Test
1. The main character.
2. A character who opposes the protagonist.
3. Something that happens to get the story going.
4. An event that changes the direction of the story.

Page 21 Quick Test
1. George lived alone.
2. Like ancient gravestones.
3. Love loyalty/apparent affection.
4. His teeth were rarely seen.

Page 23 Quick Test
1. To argue your point of view.
2. The governors. **3.** Letter.

Page 25 Quick Test
1. Yours sincerely.
2. Yours faithfully.
3. Yours faithfully.
4. Yours sincerely.

Page 26

Content and Organization

22–24	**Content:**	• You have communicated convincingly and compellingly throughout.
		• Your tone, style and register assuredly match purpose, form and audience.
		• You have used an extensive and ambitious vocabulary with sustained crafting of linguistic devices.
	Organization:	• Your writing is highly structured and developed, including a range of integrated and complex ideas.
		• Your paragraphs are fluently linked with integrated discourse markers.
		• You have used a variety of structural features in an inventive way.
19–21	**Content:**	• You have communicated convincingly.
		• Your tone, style and register consistently match purpose, form and audience.
		• You have used an extensive vocabulary with evidence of conscious crafting of linguistic devices.
	Organization:	• Your writing is structured and developed, including a range of engaging and complex ideas.
		• You have used paragraphs consistently with integrated discourse markers.
		• You have used a variety of structural features effectively.
16–18	**Content:**	• You have communicated clearly and effectively.
		• Your tone, style and register match purpose, form and audience.
		• You have used an increasingly sophisticated vocabulary with a range of appropriate linguistic devices.
	Organization:	• Your writing is engaging, including a range of engaging and detailed connected ideas.
		• You have used paragraphs coherently, with integrated discourse markers.
		• You have used structural features effectively.
13–15	**Content:**	• You have communicated clearly.
		• Your tone, style and register generally match purpose, form and audience.
		• You have used vocabulary for effect with a range of linguistic devices.
	Organization:	• Your writing is engaging, including a range of connected ideas.
		• You have usually used paragraphs coherently, with a range of discourse markers.
		• You have usually used structural features effectively.

Technical Accuracy

13–16	• You have consistently demarcated sentences accurately.
	• You have used a wide range of punctuation with a high level of accuracy.
	• You have used a full range of sentence forms for effect.
	• You have used Standard English consistently and accurately, with secure control of grammatical structures.
	• You have achieved a high level of accuracy in spelling, including ambitious vocabulary.
	• Your use of vocabulary is extensive and ambitious.
9–12	• You have usually demarcated sentences accurately.
	• You have used a range of punctuation, usually accurately.
	• You have used a variety of sentence forms for effect.
	• You have used Standard English appropriately, with control of grammatical structures.
	• You have spelled most words, including complex and irregular words, correctly.
	• Your use of vocabulary is increasingly sophisticated.

[Maximum 40 marks]

Page 27

Look at the mark scheme for page 26, decide which description is closest to your answer and then decide which mark to give yourself. This task is marked for content and organization, and for technical accuracy.

Page 28

Look at the mark scheme for page 26, decide which description is closest to your answer and then decide which mark to give yourself. This task is marked for content and organization, and for technical accuracy.

Page 29

Look at the mark scheme for page 26, decide which description is closest to your answer and then decide which mark to give yourself. This task is marked for content and organization, and for technical accuracy.

Page 30 Spelling

1. **a)** tomatoes **b)** birthdays **c)** soliloquies
   d) families **e)** parentheses **[maximum 5]**

2. **a)** **You're** not going out like that. I asked **your** sister to bring it.
   b) **There** are twenty-five people in the class. They have all done **their** homework but **they're** not sitting in the right places.
   c) Turn it off or it will **wear** out. We have no idea **where** it is but **we're** going anyway.
   d) I **passed** him in the street an hour ago. He walked right **past** me as if I wasn't there.
   e) There were only **two** exams **to** sit but that was one **too** many.
   f) If you don't go to the **practice** you'll be left out of the team. If you want to improve you will have to **practise** every day.
   [1] for each correct answer up to a maximum of [15]

Answers

3. Last **night** I went to the cinema with my friend Bob and his **father**, Michael. The whole evening was not very **successful**. The cinema was very **crowded** and we had to sit **separately**. Then, it turned out the film was in a **foreign language** and no-one could understand it. I think it was about the **environment**. Afterwards, Michael took us to a **restaurant where** we had pizzas.
    [1] for each correct answer up to a maximum of [10]

Page 31: Punctuation
1. *Great Expectations,* **[1]** one of the best-known novels by Charles Dickens, **[1]** is the story of Pip, **[1]** a boy who grows up in the marshes of Kent. At **[1]** the beginning of the story he meets an escaped convict in the churchyard where his parents are buried. **[1]**
    [maximum 5]
2. At about ten o'clock **[1]**, we went to Romio's **[1]** for pizzas. I'm **[1]** not sure what Bob's **[1]** pizza topping was but I had ham and pineapple. I wish I hadn't **[1]** because later on I was sick in Michael's **[1]** car. It's **[1]** brand new and I thought he'd **[1]** be angry but he wasn't **[1]**. We're **[1]** not going there again.   **[maximum 10]**
3. **a)** Who was that masked man? Nobody knows. **b)** The cat slept quietly on the mat; the dog slept noisily on the step. **c)** I don't believe it! That's the first answer I've got. **d)** Annie deserved the prize: she was the best baker by far. **e)** Jane and Elizabeth (the two oldest Bennet sisters) get married at the end.
    [1] for each correct answer up to a maximum of [5]

Page 32: Sentence Structure
1. **a)** complex   **b)** minor   **c)** simple
    d) compound   **e)** simple
    [1] for each correct answer up to a maximum of [5]
2. **a)** I bought Anna a bunch of flowers because it was her birthday. **[1]**
    b) He did not finish the race although they gave him a certificate. **[1]**
    a) and b) could be written with the conjunctions at the beginning of the sentence, but you would then need to add a comma after the first clause.
    c) I kept going until I reached the finishing line. **[1]**
3. Joey, who was the oldest cat in the street, never left the garden. **[1]**
4. Walking down the street, I realized I had forgotten my phone. **[1]**

Page 33: Text Structure and Organization
1. **e)** Students of Summerfield College have expressed concern about the environment they have to work in. They have a number of complaints.
    c) Jodie Collins, a spokesperson for the students, has had several meetings about the issue with the Principal. Ms Rundle apparently listened to the students' points, but later sent an email claiming that nothing can be done because of lack of funds.
    a) As a result of this, the student body has decided to appeal to the governors. Jodie has written a letter to every governor, setting out the problems as the students see them.
    d) According to this letter, students' health and safety are at risk. Among other things, toilets are not properly cleaned and standards of hygiene in the kitchen leave a lot to be desired.
    b) As yet no replies have been received. The increasingly angry students are starting to consider taking 'direct action'.
    [maximum 5]
2. **a)** When   **b)** In spite of   **c)** subsequently
    d) however   **e)** Nevertheless   **[maximum 5]**

Page 34: Standard English and Grammar
1. **a)** are   **b)** are   **c)** were   **d)** did
    e) has been   **f)** have done   **g)** were…had done
    [maximum 7]
2. **a)** pleaded   **b)** few   **c)** got   **[maximum 3]**
3. Jo: Hello. How are you? **[1]**
    Arthur: Well. Very well, thank you. **[1]**
    Jo: Do you want (*or* would you like) a drink? **[1]**
    Arthur: May I have two coffees, please? **[1]**
    Jo: Of course. Where are you sitting? **[1]**
4. I was **standing** in the street when Frankie **came** over. **[1]** I **gave** him a smile and opened **my mouth** to speak. **[1]** I was **going to** ask him how he **did** in **maths** (*or* mathematics). **[1]** I **did not say anything**. **[1] As** soon as I **saw** him I knew he **had done well**. **[1]**

Page 35: Narrative Writing
The following answers are examples of the sort of thing you might write. Your own answers will be completely different.
[1] for each reasonable answer.
1. **a)** First person; yes.
    b) Formal, using Standard English.
    c) Female; 82; Small, neat, well-dressed; Grew up on a farm and married a farmer, now living in a bungalow in a village; A widow, with two children who live abroad, friendly with the neighbours but no close friends; Speaks in a Cornish accent but uses Standard English.   **[maximum 8]**
2. **a)** In the village post office.
    b) Yes, she goes abroad.
    c) Now.   **d)** A year.
    e) Yes (except for some memories in flashback).   **[maximum 5]**
3. Exposition: Doris leads a quiet life in a small village with her two cats. Inciting incident: She wins the lottery. She decides to visit her children but not tell them she's a millionaire. Turning point: She goes to see her daughter in France, who is too busy to be bothered. She books her a ticket to Australia. In Australia her son lets her stay but after a while he puts her in a horrible home. Climax: She buys the nursing home, improves the lives of its patients and returns home, where she spends the rest of her money on herself and on charities. Coda/ending: Doris is living happily in the village with her cats and a man she met in the nursing home. She has spent all her money and not given any to her children. **[maximum 5]**

Page 36: Descriptive Writing
The following answers are examples of the sort of thing you might write. Your own answers will be completely different. **[1]** for each reasonable answer up to a maximum of **[20]** overall.
1. **a)** Third.
    b) Past.
2. **a)** Gaudy rides, milling crowds.
    b) Screeching child, loud dance music.
    c) Spicy sausage, burning wood.
    d) Tangy mustard, sweet toffee.
    e) Sticky candyfloss, slimy mud.
3. **a)** A blur of swirling colours and harsh noises.
    b) Candy-striped stall; fluffy toys piled high.
    c) Blue nylon fur, plastic brown eyes.
4. **a)** The crowd rumbled and rolled like a storm-tossed ship.
    b) An explosion of excited laughter.

Page 37: Writing Non-fiction 1 and 2

1. The following are only suggestions. There are many other points you could make. **[1]** for each up to a maximum of **[10]**.

Pros	Cons
Studying for exams is much more important.	It helps you understand the importance of things like punctuality and politeness.
The work being done is not interesting or meaningful.	It helps you choose your future career.
Students on work experience are just free labour.	You can learn new skills.
In the time you cannot get a realistic idea of what the work is like.	You might make contacts which would lead to paid employment.
You've got the rest of your life to experience work.	You get to meet a wide range of people.

2. **[1]** for each of the following up to a maximum of **[5]**:
   - opening with 'Dear Sir' or 'Dear Editor'
   - setting out the opening correctly
   - using a formal tone
   - clearly stating the purpose of your letter
   - putting your point of view strongly and clearly
   - using a rhetorical or literary device
   - accurate spelling and punctuation.

3. **[1]** for each of the following up to a maximum of **[5]**:
   - using an intriguing/amusing headline
   - using a strapline
   - using an appropriate informal tone
   - clearly stating the purpose of your article
   - putting your point of view strongly and clearly
   - using a rhetorical or literary device
   - accurate spelling and punctuation.

Notes

Notes

Notes

Notes